Rethink the Ink

Your Guide to Surviving Laser Tattoo Removal

Victor Beyer

Rethink the Ink

Printed by:
CreateSpace Independent Publishing Platform

Copyright © 2017, Victor Beyer

Published in the United States of America

ISBN-13: 978-1983710803
ISBN-10: 1983710806

For more information on 90-Minute Books including finding out how you can publish your own book, visit 90minutebooks.com or call (863) 318-0464

Here's What's Inside...

Rethink the Ink!

Today, statistics show 21% of the U.S. population is getting tattooed. Studies say as many as 50% of that 21% will, at some point in the future, have those tattoos removed. The latest statistics on Millennials show that at least 40% of Millennials have tattoos; of that 40%, 40% have two or more tattoos.

Gone are the days when tattoos were only for a subculture of people. People everywhere are getting them to mark milestones in their lives or to honor loved ones. As more and more people get tattoos, it's only natural that more and more people will want their tattoos removed.

The removal process is how I found myself in the industry years ago. Since then, I've witnessed the horror stories of tattoos gone wrong and what can happen when someone who doesn't know what they are doing tries to remove a tattoo.

I'm passionate about getting the word out on how to safely and correctly remove a tattoo. I've become well aware of many of the perils and pitfalls people fall into when removing tattoos; it's the reason I wanted to write this book.

Unlike most books on tattoos, which come from the clinic's perspective, the client's perspective, or the practitioner's perspective, this book will cover all bases. Everyone who picks up this book will be fully aware of the full process, no matter what angle they're coming from.

Enjoy the book!

I hope this book inspires you to complete the tattoo removal process, but in the safest way possible.

To Your Success!

Victor Beyer

Why Some People Want to Remove Their Tattoos

Most people completely misunderstand the tattoo-removal industry. When they think about someone with a tattoo, they immediately imagine someone who is probably a male with images of dragons and heavy metal on their skin. In reality, 80% of our clients are female, and the top reasons they want to get their tattoos removed are divorce, a breakup, or a pregnancy. The top reasons for males are divorce and children for females.

Regret is another reason people want to remove their tattoos. A person is much different at 40 years old than they were at 20. As people go through different stages of life, they sometimes like to erase chapters or memories they once wanted to memorialize.

Tattoos also often get removed when a person enters the professional world. Maybe they were a landscaper from 18 to 21 to put themselves through college, and they put on some tattoos during that stage of their life. Now they're 26 and have a chance to enter the professional world and would like their tattoo removed.

The military is also a major motivator for tattoo removal. The military's regulations change all the time. Each branch also has different regulations, and some branches don't allow tattoos. The same is true for police and fire departments. In some parts of the country, police and fire departments are very conservative, while others are a bit more liberal. Departments that are conservative, typically, don't like to see any tattoos from the elbows down.

Sadly, another reason why women get tattoos removed is they were branded when previously working in the sex industry. Someone marked them with a tattoo to show whose property they were. In other situations, women are branded by ex-boyfriends or husbands who tattoo them to make sure the man's name or mark is all over the woman's body.

Tattoo removal is a misunderstood process, especially in the medical community. At one point, tattoo removal was stigmatized, and medical offices didn't want anything to do with it. Most tattoo artists believe that once a tattoo is applied, it's there for life. Over the last five to eight years, the tattoo industry has finally come to realize that removal goes hand-in-hand with tattooing. Tattoo removal is the process of doing a tattoo in reverse.

When I was 17 and just coming out of the military boot camp, I had a typical grim reaper which was about the size of a watermelon and tattooed near my left shoulder on my back. At 28, when I had my daughter, I realized I didn't want to have to explain what the grim reaper meant or represented when she was able to talk and have a conversation with me.

I started tattoo-removal treatments and became interested in how they did it. I went to a clinic to research the different processes and methods. After my schooling, I opened my own clinic.

Changing a Chapter in One's Life

Most people don't understand that a tattoo is a chapter in someone's life. That person will remember the date and the time of the tattoo, the smell of the studio, the artist's name, and exactly why they wanted that chapter memorialized on their body. Tattoos are much deeper than most people who don't have tattoos realize. They have meaning and personality.

Why does that matter for the removal process? When I do a removal, I have to do that process in reverse. At one point, the person in my clinic was super stoked and happy, looking forward to memorializing that moment and about to make a commitment forever. On the removal side, something has changed internally, so the person wants that chapter to disappear.

The general rule in tattoo removal is to never ask clients why they want their tattoos removed; doing so can get into touchy, personal, squishy feelings that don't need to be brought up. Ninety-nine percent of the time, clients or customers are more than happy to explain why they want their tattoos removed, but the general rule of thumb is to never ask them.

A big misconception about tattoo removal is that it scars. In the right hands, there should be zero scarring. Unfortunately, there's a lot of misinformation about tattoo removal which I will address later in this book.

Tattoo removal started in the early 1990s. There was some experimentation prior to that, but in the early '90s, wavelengths were used to remove tattoos. There was not much knowledge as to how wavelengths interacted with the skin, so results were poor when using this method for tattoo removal. A person could get 30 or more treatments, and color still wasn't able to be removed.

In the 2000s, the number of treatments in the removal process decreased, and the ability to target color improved. Overall, the process got better, but there was still a good chance of scarring.

In today's world of tattoo removal, we can target full color. On average, a person has eight to ten treatments, and there is no reason a client would be scarred.

One of my very first clients was a young gentleman who had just lost his father. He had memorialized his dad's passing on his neck in the form of a tattoo which was very visible from the left side of his neck up to his chin. He quickly realized he was unable to find employment because of his tattoo. He was a very high-end cabinet-maker, but none of the high-end cabinet-makers in town wanted to hire him or put him on a job site with that tattoo.

When he came to me, he was very emotional. He loved his dad, but he needed to make the decision to remove his tattoo, so he could make a living and support his family.

The Tattoo Removal Process

The industry is full of a lot of mistruths which stem from both practitioners and manufacturers of the devices themselves. For instance, most people don't understand that the ink of a tattoo is in a semi-liquid form in the skin. When a removal is done, that ink is turned into a solid and then broken into tiny pieces. The body is lymphatic; its macrophages digest the ink.

There are two things we don't know going into this process, no matter who walks through the door. First, we don't know what inks a client is tattooed with. The FDA (Food and Drug Administration) does not regulate inks, so they can be comprised of a plethora of ingredients.

Today's inks are very sophisticated, and almost every single one is based in metal salts. Most practitioners and most clients who have red ink do not know that reds contain mercury and cinnabar. Thirty percent of the general public is allergic to red ink at the time of installation. If we turn the laser on somebody who's had an allergic reaction to mercury and cinnabar, they can have a very adverse reaction when we attempt to remove that red ink.

The other thing we don't know is the details of our client's immune system. Fifty percent of tattoo-removal success depends on the body's ability to carry away the ink through the lymphatic channel, and 50% depends on the technology the client is treated with.

For example, smoking cigarettes reduces the body's ability to complete the removal process by 70% because smoking is so hard on the body's immune system. Along with smoking, drinking and lifestyle also play a role.

Another consideration is the practitioner and the equipment. How good was the treatment, and how well did the practitioner understand how to remove the tattoo?

When someone gets a tattoo, they need to stay out of the sun. The same applies to the removal process. If someone doesn't heed that advice, they will get the biggest blisters they've ever seen and experience hypopigmentation, when the melanin is stripped out of the dermis. This is very hard to fix.

The Fitzpatrick Scale was founded by a dermatologist named Dr. Thomas B. Fitzpatrick, and it's based on the body's ability to deal with UV (ultraviolet) light. Skin Type I in tattoo removal is albino, which is very rare. Skin Type Six is blue-black. A person with Skin Type VI is so black, they're blue. People with this skin type are typically from Kenya. Everybody else falls in between these extremes.

The Fitzpatrick Scale is very important in tattoo removal because it correlates with the principles of light: Light reflects, and black absorbs. When I use a medical device to shatter pigment, I should note whether I'm affecting pigment in the tattoo or pigment in the natural dermis. The laser does not care; it searches for color.

One of the side effects in certain skin types is hypopigmentation; taking the melanin out of the dermis, which is why the Fitzpatrick Scale is important. I like to teach people that Fitzpatrick is like a canvas, and the practitioner is the painter; they have to look at the painting.

Practitioners often get the Fitzpatrick Scale wrong when it comes to being very fair. They're taught that being fair is good, which is a solid general rule, but people with Skin Type II are redheads, who typically come with freckles. The typical practitioner turns the laser up because the client looks fair, but they don't pay attention to their freckles. Freckles are melanin, and melanin absorbs, which heightens the client's chances of getting hurt. They get blistered or scarred because the practitioner didn't pay attention to their background. The client also doesn't get the results they want.

Another side effect is hyperpigmentation, which is the darkening of the skin. This is very easy to fix. Hyperpigmentation occurs when the body senses trauma and sends too much melanin to an area. If it's left alone, it will calm down, and the melanin will disperse.

Hypopigmentation, on the other hand, is very hard to fix. Think of Michael Jackson; he started off one shade and basically lost his natural color.

Most people in this industry and almost every client who comes in for removal doesn't know that once someone is tattooed, the ink lies in three different positions in the dermis. Blacks and grays sit up against the subcutaneous layer, where tissue meets skin. Blues and greens sit mid-skin. They're still in the dermis, but near the very top. Any colors in the red family, yellows, and oranges reside in the top layer of the dermis, known as the epidermis.

Why is this important to know? In the world of lasers, there has to be a relevancy to the nanometer interacting with the inks, and the different depths in which those inks reside. Most practitioners don't know this fact, and because they don't know this fact, they don't know how to properly remove a tattoo at the end of the process. It's incredibly important to understand where inks reside in the dermis; in relation to the dermis and the epidermis. Clients looking for tattoo removal should know this information as well.

Blacks are the easiest colors to remove. We now have the ability to remove blues and greens, but they get darker before they lighten. Of all the colors, reds are the easiest to remove.

As far as an overall experience, there's absolutely no reason a practitioner should blister somebody. Blistering does not mean a better treatment. It increases the chances of infections and wounds. Blistering is actually a sign of over-treatment.

When practitioners work with a nanosecond laser, known as a Q-switch, they heat the ink up to over 900 degrees in a billionth of a second. For this reason, it's important for clients to seek out clinicians who are well-versed. Practitioners should remember they're working with their clients' skin, heating it up to over 900 degrees in a billionth of a second.

In general, the newer the tattoo; the definition of "new" being no older than 10 years; the slower the removal process will be. If a tattoo is 10 years old or older, the body has had time to digest it; to work at it with macrophages. This is why an 80-year-old sailor's arm is unrecognizable. The body's macrophages have had time to remove the ink. The older the tattoo, the easier is it to remove.

The closer we work to the neck, the better the results. This is because what makes a tattoo permanent is the size of the ink molecule in relation to the macrophages, which are very, very tiny. When someone gets a cold, those cleanser cells engulf the germs and then run them through the lymphatic system and they're expelled through waste.

Tattoo removal is easier as a tattoo gets older because the body and the macrophages have had time to digest the ink. This is also why older tattoos lose their luster and look faded. The body is naturally digesting it. Tattoo removal takes this natural process and speeds it up.

For the most part, tattoos are permanent, but tattoo artists know that tattoos in the reds family don't last very long. As I mentioned, red inks lie in the epidermis, and the epidermis exfoliates. Whites sit on top of everything, so they don't last more than five to sometimes 15 years because the body exfoliates the color away. Blues, greens, and blacks are most permanent because they lie in the dermis.

I had two clients with tattoos of about the same age, both under a year old. One client was a Brazilian mixed martial arts (MMA) fighter, and the other was Russian. I removed the tattoo of the MMA fighter in three treatments. He had probably 4% to 5% body fat because, as an MMA fighter, he trained six days a week.

My Russian client had essentially the same tattoo; with even a little less ink; and I did approximately 23 treatments. She smoked three packs of cigarettes a day and drank like a fish. That put such a drag on her immune system that it took 23 or more treatments to get her tattoo remotely removed. That's how big an impact lifestyle has on removal.

The DOs and DON'Ts of Tattoo Removal

The biggest takeaway of this book is for the practitioner to find out where their client got their tattoo; not the location on the body, but where the installation process took place, geographically. All inks in North America have zero FDA regulation, and some people, service members especially are tattooed overseas, perhaps in a third-world country. The ink in their body could have some really bad components. One of the most common practices is to boil off toner ink in third-world countries and use that for tattooing.

Clients who know they were tattooed in a not-so-friendly place should keep an eye on their tattoo removal for rashes or unusual reactions after the process. This does not include blistering or anything that's part of the treatment, but they might see aggravation around the area as their immune system reacts to the release of the toxins in the bad ink.

In the age of the Internet, it's very difficult to decipher who is a good practitioner, who's bad, and who has the best equipment. Here is a very easy way to find someone proficient: Look at before-and-after pictures. They reveal a lot.

When a before-and-after image shows remnants of a tattoo, it's called ghosting. If the tattoo is still clearly visible, and the practitioner claims they're proficient, they are in no way proficient. They're misleading and should be avoided.

It's also important to confirm that before-and-after images actually belong to the clinic claiming them. A good way of knowing is to look for the watermark of the clinic's logo, the doctor's name, or the practitioner's name. With one simple right click, someone could copy another practitioner's work and claim it's theirs. Unfortunately, that is very common in this industry.

Secondly, it's incredibly important to read reviews. A clinic with three five-star reviews is probably not the best choice. A clinic running 50 to 100 reviews is a better choice. Reliable places to find reviews are on Yelp and Google; Bing and Yahoo aren't as commonly used.

If a clinic received a bad review, it's important to note how they responded. Did they address the client's concerns? Was the poor review simply due to an employee problem or a miscommunication? If a clinic doesn't address a problem at all, that tells me they're not really concerned about the client. We've become so successful in tattoo removal because all we do is care about clients and their results. The reviews take care of themselves because we satisfy clients' removal needs.

A person coming in for removal should not opt for the first deal that pops up on the Internet, like Groupons, 30%, buy-one-get-one-free Tuesday tattoo removal, $15 special. They still need to do their research. If the clinic's "before-and-afters" and reviews check out, and there's a deal, that's great, but it's not a good idea to jump on the very first clinic that offers removal.

Someone searching for removal should also visit lots of clinics. On the clinic's side, their money is made not during treatments, but in informing clients how the process works. Tattoo removal is a subscription business. I typically see my clients eight to ten times to provide my services and get the removal process done. Spending time to help the client understand the process has three benefits: better results, a longer life of the client, and much better chances of them staying on board and finishing the process.

In addition to reading reviews, looking at "before-and-after" pictures and visiting lots of clinics, somebody getting a removal should research the clinic's equipment because many practitioners were misinformed when they purchased their lasers. The machine used should provide a full removal process with zero scarring.

Moreover, just because a clinic claims to have the latest technology does not mean they do. Technology in tattoo removal evolves every three years. The latest version of tattoo technology is currently out on the market, but unfortunately, the latest and greatest is scarring a tremendous number of people and not doing what the laser manufacturer promised with some colors. If the client takes five minutes to research the quality of a clinic's equipment, they should look for Q-switch lasers, which do pigmented lesions, removing color.

To really know this, a person has to research a particular clinic practitioner. How much experience do they have? Do they do this every day? Many practitioners in this business may turn the laser on once every Thursday or every other Tuesday. There are also mobile tattoo-removal services which stop by a physician's office every other week. A good clinic does tattoo removal exclusively. We have a motto: "Tattoo removal. It's not something we do. It's all we do" because that's all we do every day: deal with different inks, different skin types, different body locations, different ages, and different medications. We get the results our clients desire.

Once someone finds a clinic they're happy with and is ready to start the removal process, they should not buy a full removal package, which is when a clinic, practitioner or physician says they will remove a tattoo for one set price. A practitioner might say, "I'll remove that grape-sized tattoo on your ribs for $3,200, no matter how many treatments it takes."

Again, there are two things we don't know: your immune system and what inks you're tattooed with. We get a general idea in the beginning, especially after the first treatment, how quickly your body's going to remove it. Treatments are spaced four weeks apart, minimally.

A very well-known physician in Southern California with multiple branches of clinics charged one standard fee for removal processes. Clients did have the option to pay treatment to treatment, but the clinic made the bulk of its money by selling flat-fee treatments, no matter how many treatments it took.

The physician sold a lot of $2,000 to $10,000 packages and then claimed bankruptcy and is now out of business. I have clients who have funneled into our clinics from that practice. One of my clients, unfortunately, paid $8,000 and received two treatments only to be hit with bankruptcy papers.

Another thing to avoid during the entire course of treatment is UV exposure to the treated area. There should be no UV exposure whatsoever.

Aftercare is simple but very important. Clients shouldn't get caught up in buying a bunch of lotions and potions for aftercare. Aftercare for removal is very similar to care after getting a tattoo: It shouldn't be exposed to any UV light, and nothing should be put on the area during the whole course of treatments because the body needs to see the broken ink and not any specialized products that are being administered. This will ensure a fast and quick clean-up of those broken ink particles.

Drinking lots of water is also very simple but very important.

Lasers: The Right Tool for the Job

A very simplified, Q-switch laser works by exciting an atom. The atom then falls asleep or dies off, and that produces a photon. We capture the photons in the laser in two mirrors and then release them during treatment through a solid-state crystal. Depending on what the solid-state crystal is; we call them the Nd YAG, the ruby; when we cut that in half, known as 532 KTP. They're known as nanometers. Photons vibrate as they go through the atmosphere, and we measure those vibrations in a nanometer. The higher the nanometer registers, the deeper the penetration will be. When we go after black ink, we use a wavelength called 1064, known as the Nd YAG or the YAG in the industry. It penetrates 1,064 nanometers into the dermis, to the deepest spot, where black inks reside.

To target blue and green inks, we put those photons through an actual ruby crystal which produces 694 nanometers and goes mid-skin, exactly where the blues and greens reside.

To go after reds, we cut 1,064 in half, known as frequency doubling and use a wavelength called 532. Reds sit in the epidermis, and 532 nanometers is a very shallow wavelength, so it works in the epidermis. When we fire a 532, it's the brightest green light because opposites attract. The opposite color to red on the spectrum is green, so the green laser is attracted to the red ink. The 532 wavelength also sees and interacts with hemoglobin; your blood.

As an overview, when we use a laser, we're capturing photons and putting them through a crystal, which generates the nanometers. We use the nanometers to go to the depth needed to interact with the colors, shattering the most ink and getting the best results.

There are two forms of light: Gaussian profile and top-hat profile. Gaussian translates to circular light. Light comes from the end of the laser shaped like a tennis ball. This is older technology. Tennis balls don't go on tennis balls very well. The technician has to overlap 30% to compensate for older technology. If a traffic cone were turned upside down, that's exactly the way the light penetrates the skin, producing hot spots. Gaussian treatment hurts more, can cause more damage, and prolongs healing time.

The new technology for delivering light is top-hat profile. It looks like a 1880s top hat; the kind gentlemen used to wear. This is what goes into the skin, just turned upside-down. The light is square, and squares go next to squares easily during the treatment, so there is no overlap. This light produces no hot spots and is easier on the skin. It takes one to three weeks to heal after Gaussian profile, and top-hat profile takes just three hours because it shatters a lot more ink.

Pico technology is still a Q-switch laser, but the timing is finer. A traditional Q-switch laser fires in a nanosecond or one billionth of a second. A Pico laser fires in a picosecond or one trillionth of a second. That's a hugely different amount of time. Many practitioners and manufacturers claim firing light a lot faster to break up the ink delivers better results. However, they're missing the fact that it fires so fast it generates a lot more heat in the dermis, which scars more easily.

When a tattoo is administered, each pass of the machine deposits ink about the width of a human hair. A gray wash tattoo, for instance, is very light; it doesn't have high ink density. A tribal tattoo, on the other hand, has very high density. If the tattoo machine deposits ink the width of a human hair, a tribal tattoo requires a lot of hair to be broken up. The higher the ink density, the more heat needs to be generated.

Someone who has heavy ink content needs to find a highly experienced practitioner to remove their tattoo because they're quite easy to hurt. That comes in the side of lasers because if you get in the hands of the wrong technology where the count of time, especially being a higher skin type, you're going to absorb all the pulses more. Again, white reflects, and black absorbs. Generating more heat increases the client's chances of being hurt.

In addition to the fact that denser ink makes it easier for the client to get hurt in the wrong hands, practitioners need to consider details like Gaussian profile versus top-hat profile versus wavelengths. Clinics and practitioners have been told certain wavelengths can remove full color when they might only get a 30% reduction.

For all these reasons, it's important for both practitioners and clients to be well-informed, do their due diligence, and understand how the removal process works.

I've opened hundreds of clinics all over North America and taught people from around the world. As a clinic owner, I look at my work that involves working with somebody's skin as a calling card. My worst nightmare is hurting a client. My clinics have done thousands and thousands of removals, and we've never scarred a soul.

When I fly around the world, teaching people and opening clinics, I get frustrated hearing the same stories: A lot of people get hurt when they have tattoos removed because the practitioner or clinic lacks care, the practitioner or client misunderstands how the process works, or the client doesn't care for the area properly after the removal. Some people pick or scratch at the site. I've even had clients use sandpaper, a TCA peel, or hydrochloric acid to try to expedite the process. It's a natural process, and people need to have patience.

I was recently featured in a film called *D-Inked*, which premiered in LA. The gentleman sitting to my left during the premier was also featured in the film. He had taken TCA to his face to remove some flames around his mustache and chin region and gave himself a bad chemical burn. The TCA removed some of the tattoo and then decided a bit later to try a soldering iron. He filmed himself using a soldering iron on his face.

There are two alternatives to lasers in the world of tattoo removal. The tattoo can either be cut out, or dermabrasion can be used. Cutting out a tattoo is known as excision, it's performed by a physician, and it's almost guaranteed to scar. In a dermabrasion treatment, a physician sands off the tattoo, which, again, leads to scarring.

I'm tired of seeing people hurt. In every part of North America I've been to, I have come across clients who are scarred and banged up. Lasers are really the only true option for removal. Practitioners need to take pride in what they do and take care of their clients. Clients also need to take care of themselves; avoid picking it and using alternative processes.

Common Practice Mistakes

Often, clinics don't look out for clients' best interests. If, for instance, they see a client who would like six tattoos removed because he needs to get into the military or just went through a breakup, they treat the client like a wallet and offer to remove all six today for a certain amount of money.

Doing removal all over the body can actually slow down the process because the body gets confused. It doesn't know where to send the cleanser cells. Clients should never be treated like wallets.

Clients should concentrate on one or two tattoos at most. When I say two tattoos, the size of combined ink should not exceed the size of a dollar bill. This will help maximize the process and give the client the biggest bang for their buck. Doing treatments all over the body will slow the process down.

In my experience, doctors (MDs); especially derms and plastics; tend to be the biggest offenders when it comes to bad practice. Just because someone has "MD" behind their name does not mean they're proficient at their craft. I've seen the most scarring from these "experts." They also tend to think if they do hurt a client, they will fix them with plastic surgery or their practice of medicine. I don't find that acceptable in any form.

MDs who do tattoo removal need to take the time to dive deeper into the process. They need to understand more about the inks and that they're generating 900 degrees in pigment that's based in metal, so it will conduct heat. They need to understand the three locations of ink and that deeper in the dermis contains more water and tissue, which disperses and better handles heat. When removing blues and greens mid-skin, it's easier to blister somebody, and reds are incredibly easy to blister because where they sit in the skin contains no water and tissue to disperse the heat and because the color is very heavily based in metal salts. Practitioners must understand where they're working in the skin.

The purpose of a consult is to educate the client because they need to understand the process and how it depends on their body. At a minimum, treatments need to be four weeks apart, but some clients smoke or have compromised immune systems. Those clients should not come in every four weeks. The proper thing to do is give them more time in between treatments. We space some of our clients out 6, 8, 10, or 12 weeks. Some of them get six months between treatments because their bodies move the ink slowly.

Clients should not be afraid to ask their practitioners if they're moving the ink at a proficient rate. A clinic should be able to look at the number of treatments a client has had, their progress so far, before and after results and determine if they're moving ink. If a clinic can't answer that question, I would advise a client to find another clinic that can.

It's very common for practitioners not to know how to assess tattoos. I highly suggest they spend some time at a tattoo studio, learning the process of tattooing. It's a true art form, and many studios are changing to reflect that. They're becoming actual art galleries, with wine tastings and artwork sales in addition to providing tattoos. There are some incredibly talented tattoo artists out there.

A removal practitioner needs to understand what they're looking at when they look at a tattoo. How clean is the line work? Are there blown-out lines? Are they feathery? They need to be able to assess whether a tattoo was done by an apprentice, a true professional, or a scratcher. In the community, we're taught that the more amateurish a tattoo is, the easier it should be to remove. That's false because a tattoo machine in the wrong hands can scar a client and make the removal process that much harder. Practitioners need to take the time to understand.

They should also ask clients; especially those who have prison tattoos, what the ink was mixed with. Many practitioners just do treatments, but today's jailhouse tattoos are mixed with a plethora of carrier solutions.

In prison, they sometimes take whatever will be the pigment; typically the sole of a shoe or a rubber band and burn it to make it a powder. Then they need something to carry it into the body. This is sometimes urine or baby oil. Urine is sterile, hence why it's used in tattooing and will remove very easily.

A practitioner needs to ask what a jailhouse tattoo consists of. If toothpaste and shampoo were used, for instance, that's a problem. Toothpaste and shampoo are primarily whites and contain plastics and polymers. Firing a laser at 900 degrees into that mixture re-emulsifies the plastics and polymers into the client, hurting them.

Clients should not be afraid to give their practitioners detailed information about their tattoos because it only helps achieve the goal of removal.

A very common mistake clinics make is overpromising and under-delivering. Because of new technology, the hottest trend has been to tell clients they can get fewer treatments, usually four to six. Again, if a practitioner doesn't know the client's immune system or the inks they're tattooed with, they can't promise that. If I could do treatments in four to six weeks, I would be a super wealthy guy, but that's not the way this business works.

A lot of clinics try to get savvy and promise certain things and then find themselves in a quandary when the fourth treatment has passed, and the tattoo hasn't shown any changes. They find themselves in panic mode, and the client is frustrated because they were promised something and it wasn't delivered. Again, a practitioner's experience is so important.

For some reason, people believe they've won the lottery when they purchase a laser. It's tempting because there are not too many jobs where someone can charge $99 to $150 for a minute's worth of work and make good money. Lasers are expensive, and the biggest mistake I see people coming into this industry make is using their life savings to purchase a laser. A lot of physicians do this, too. They purchase the laser, think they've hit the lottery, and buy a facility with seven treatment rooms and one laser. Or they spend all their money getting the laser and forget they have to market their services and actually furnish their clinic with computers and phones.

A clinic in northern Colorado went into business with seven treatment rooms. The owner put all his money into the business, but his waiting room had patio furniture because he had spent all his money acquiring a laser and thought the profits would just roll in.

Practitioners starting businesses or looking to acquire new equipment should remember this is the same as any other industry. A person has to work hard, understand what they're doing, put it into practice, and become very proficient. Simply owning a laser will not make someone a millionaire.

The Cold Hard Truth

Let's get into some of the cold, hard truths about the practitioner side. The biggest myth is that this process takes one treatment. We average eight to ten treatments.

A practitioner coming out of school with a huge amount of knowledge still requires two years tattoo-removal experience every day before I consider them proficient. Doing tattoo removals is like being a cop: They don't know what's going to come through the door every day. It takes a tremendous amount of treatments for a practitioner to understand the process. Clients should find clinics that have been doing this for longer than two years.

Clients looking for removal need to understand it takes time because, again, it depends on their bodies. The laser is not a magic wand. I like to say meta-aesthetics is like Hawaii: It might be paradise, but there are snakes in the grass. Every industry has undesirables, and tattoo removal probably has a lot more than I would consider the average. Every single laser manufacturer and clinic claims they're the best. Clients need to review their "before-and-afters", their track record, who they are, their education, and with whom they're associated.

Clients should also understand that practitioners will find out if they have cover-ups or a new tattoo over an old tattoo that they're trying to hide. It's not worth trying to say they don't have it because a practitioner will find it in the removal process. They need to know that information because it's not one tattoo removal; it's two, which means more treatments.

Clients looking for removal should be truthful with their practitioners. Practitioners see embarrassing, compromising things on a daily basis, and they will see what clients try to hide. We have a saying: "The laser will tell us the truth when the clients will not."

The cold, hard truth about laser companies is they don't care two cents about practitioners. Practitioners should not buy into laser companies saying they'll take care of marketing or running the business or show how to do something. At the end of the day, they have one job to do: sell a laser and then be down the road selling the next one.

Practitioners looking to renegotiate their lasers or purchase lasers should slow the process down and take their time. Everything is negotiable. Laser companies are not friends with practitioners. They aren't going to reveal some mythical, magical way to make lots of money. Their one job is to sell a laser and then move on to the next client. Sales reps of laser manufacturers typically know nothing about the process, and what they do know is usually misleading.

Research is crucial for both clients and practitioners. The biggest cold, hard truth is that people get misled. If a practitioner doesn't know the answer to a client's question, they should pick up the phone and find somebody who can help. If a client has a question, they should search around until they find somebody who gives them the proper information without spinning a story.

People in the industry should never spin stories because it makes it hard to keep up with clients.

There Is Hope: Tips and Tricks

Females should not have removal treatments done during their time of the month. During that week, females have heightened sensitivity, so it's not an enjoyable experience.

Almost everyone experiences some pain or discomfort. At our clinics, we call it "spice." There's a little spice when we do removals, but most removals take less than two minutes to perform.

If someone has a morning appointment, especially females, they should eat in the morning. Everyone needs to have a little something in their system before they come in because the process causes an endorphin dump, which can make them a little woozy. It's the same as tattooing.

The client should not have any sun exposure two weeks prior to treatment.

Having a test spot done is an option. That's when a client comes in for a consult, and we perform a treatment on an area about the size of an eraser on a pencil. It's just one or two quick pulses to see how the dermis and the body in general react. That's when clients quickly understand why we call it a little spice. Spice is needed with discomfort in the treatment. A test spot is a great way to see if it's a proper fit and should be done at no charge.

Rethink the Ink Call-to-Action

There are two primary ways for clients looking for tattoo removal to work with us: They can look at our website **www.RethinktheInk.com**, or they can give us a call and talk to me or anyone on my staff. We are more than happy to answer questions, and we even do online consults for free. We're here to help.

We can be reached at **(800) 677-8435** to talk about tattoo removal.

Practitioners looking to get caught up on the latest, greatest technique; how to avoid blisters; how to understand this process in much more depth for maximized results; how to get happier clients; and how to generate more cash flow should know we have a track record with the people we have taught which sets the bar in the industry. We've been featured in film and magazines. I'm a featured speaker on the medical circuit. We're the only school in the world that teaches tattoo inks in depth and how that relates to the removal process.

Practitioners can reach us at **www.alaseracademy.com**, where they'll find a lot of information. They can also pick up the phone, if they have questions, and give us a call: **(800) 221-6721**.

Here's How to Safely and Effectively Have Your Tattoo Removed

You've always wanted to remove your tattoo, but you are scared of scarring and whether or not the process will even work.

That's where we come in. We help people just like you receive safe and effective tattoo-removal treatments.

Here are three ways we can help you right now:

Option 1: If you are looking to have a tattoo removed, call us at **(800) 677-8435** for a free consultation. We'll educate you and find out more information about your tattoo. We'll answer all your questions about the process and work with you until your tattoo is completely gone.

Option 2: Like us on **Facebook/RethinktheInk**, or follow us on **Twitter @RethinktheInk** to stay up-to-date on the tattoo removal process and industry.

Option 3: If you are a studio owner and desire better outcomes and happier clients, contact **A Laser Academy** at **www.ALaserAcademy.com**, or call us at **(800) 221-6721**.

Most people at one point consider or wonder if they could remove a tattoo, but they aren't sure of their options or if it will work for them.

Now, you can safely and effectively have your tattoo removed, and it's easier than you think.

If you'd like our help, give us as all at **(800) 677-8435**, and we'll take it from there.

www.ingramcontent.com/pod-product-compliance
Lightning Source LLC
Chambersburg PA
CBHW050708250726
48662CB00002B/903